IN JUN 2009

Shia LaBeouf

ABDO
Publishing Company

A Big Buddy Book
by **Sarah Tieck**

VISIT US AT
www.abdopublishing.com

Published by ABDO Publishing Company, 8000 West 78th Street, Edina, Minnesota 55439.

Copyright © 2009 by Abdo Consulting Group, Inc. International copyrights reserved in all countries. No part of this book may be reproduced in any form without written permission from the publisher. Buddy Books™ is a trademark and logo of ABDO Publishing Company.

Printed in the United States.

Coordinating Series Editor: Rochelle Baltzer
Contributing Editors: Heidi M.D. Elston, Megan M. Gunderson, Marcia Zappa
Graphic Design: Maria Hosley
Cover Photograph: AP Photo: Richard Drew
Interior Photographs/Illustrations: AP Photo: Jae C. Hong (page 11), Danny Moloshok (page 25), Jack Plunkett (page 29), Chris Polk (page 24), Matt Sayles (pages 13, 27), Miranda Shen (page 18), Mark J. Terrill (pages 5, 16, 23); Getty Images: WireImage/Bobby Bank (page 26), WireImage for Paramount Pictures - CA/Eric Charbonneau (page 21), WireImage/Harold Cunningham (page 23), WireImage/Gregg de Guire (page 7), Lucy Nicholson (page 15), WireImage/Jeff Vespa (page 6), Kevin Winter (pages 9, 19); iStockphoto: earntsen (page 13); Photos.com (page 17).

Library of Congress Cataloging-in-Publication Data

Tieck, Sarah, 1976-
  Shia LaBeouf / Sarah Tieck.
     p. cm. -- (Big buddy biographies)
  Includes index.
  ISBN 978-1-60453-123-7
  1. LaBeouf, Shia, 1986---Juvenile literature. 2. Actors--United States--Biography--Juvenile literature. I. Title.

  PN2287.L12T54 2009
  792.02'8092--dc22
  [B]
                              2008009363

Shia LaBeouf

Contents

Rising Star

Shia LaBeouf is an actor. He has appeared in television shows and movies. Shia is best known for starring in *Even Stevens*, *Holes*, and *Transformers*.

The funny television show *Even Stevens* was Shia's breakout role. Since then, he has done more serious acting work.

Oregon

California · Nevada

PACIFIC OCEAN

Burbank
Los Angeles · Arizona

MEXICO

Family Ties

Shia Saide LaBeouf was born on June 11, 1986, in Los Angeles, California. His parents are Jeffrey and Shayna LaBeouf. Shia is an only child.

Did you know...

Shia has the same first name as his grandfather. It is Hebrew for "gift from god."

Shia's parents often attend events with him.

7

A Young Actor

People noticed Shia's talent for performing when he was just three! His first acting job was performing in an Oreo **commercial**. By age 12, Shia began working **professionally** as a **comedian**.

At first, Shia became an actor to help his family earn money.

In 1998, Shia made his television **debut**. He had a **role** on a show called *Breakfast with Einstein*. Starting in 2000, Shia starred in the Disney Channel's *Even Stevens*. On the show, he played Louis Stevens. *Even Stevens* is about Louis and his sister's playful friendship. Shia's role helped people notice him.

In 2003, Shia won a Daytime Emmy Award for his work on *Even Stevens*. Receiving this American television award is a big honor! Shia has received many other awards for his acting.

School Days

During his younger years, Shia rarely attended a regular school. Instead, he worked with private teachers.

Shia was a good student. After high school, he was accepted to Yale University in Connecticut. But, Shia decided to continue acting instead.

Shia took classes at 32nd Street/USC Visual and
Performing Arts Magnet School. He also briefly attended
Alexander Hamilton High School. Both are in Los Angeles.

Yale University is considered one
of the best colleges in the world.

13

First Movie

After *Even Stevens* ended in 2003, Shia starred in his first movie. It was a Disney film called *Holes*. Shia played Stanley "Caveman" Yelnats IV.

Many people liked Shia's work in *Holes*. This helped him get more movie **roles**.

Shia and Khleo Thomas star in *Holes*. The movie is about a camp for kids who break the law. The kids must dig giant holes every day!

Jon Voight is a well-known actor. He played Mr. Sir in *Holes*.

For parts of *Holes*, Shia worked in a desert. Sometimes it was very hot!

While working on *Holes*, Shia became friends with his costar Jon Voight. Jon taught Shia about acting. This changed Shia's ideas about being an actor. He realized acting could be more than a job.

New Opportunities

Later in 2003, Shia appeared on HBO's *Project Greenlight*. The show is about the making of a movie. The movie is called *The Battle of Shaker Heights*.

In 2004, Shia bought a home in Burbank, California. Over the next few years, Shia acted in more movies. He had **roles** in *Charlie's Angels: Full Throttle* and *The Greatest Game Ever Played*. He was also in *I, Robot*.

In 2004, Shia attended the opening of *I, Robot*. There, people could see the special car Audi created for the movie.

In 2004, Shia helped write and direct *Let's Love Hate*. It won two children's short film awards.

Josh Fitter was one of Shia's costars in *The Greatest Game Ever Played*.

In 2007, Shia had **roles** in several successful movies. He was the voice of Cody Maverick, a penguin, in *Surf's Up*. And, he received many positive reviews for his role in *Disturbia*.

turbia

A Turning Point

In 2007, Shia's biggest **role** was in *Transformers*. He had grown up watching *Transformers* cartoons. So, he was excited to be part of the movie.

Shia exercised to get strong enough to play his part. He then performed some of his own **stunts** in the movie!

In *Transformers*, Shia played a smart teenager named Sam Witwicky. Sam helps the Autobots fight against the Decepticons.

Shia's successful movies
have won him many fans.

Transformers was very popular. The first week it was released, it made more than $150 million! That was more than any other movie earned that week.

Transformers was also successful **internationally**. This success made many people notice Shia's acting skills. Soon, he was getting even more important movie **roles**.

Some people have compared Shia to popular actor Tom Hanks. Tom is known for his acting talent.

Did you know...

Indiana Jones is a professor who goes on adventures to find treasures. Shia plays his son, Mutt.

There are many unsafe stunts in the Indiana Jones movies. During dangerous scenes, stunt doubles performed Shia and Harrison Ford's roles. Stunt doubles have skills that help them stay safe.

In 2008, Shia starred in *Indiana Jones and the Kingdom of the Crystal Skull*. He got to work with famous director Steven Spielberg.

This is the fourth Indiana Jones movie. The first three were very popular. So, many people were excited to see the newest one.

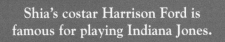
Shia's costar Harrison Ford is famous for playing Indiana Jones.

Buzz

Shia continues to make movies. In 2008, he began work on *Eagle Eye*. The young star also agreed to star in *Transformers 2*. Many believe Shia LaBeouf has a bright **future**.

Shia is serious about his work. Many people have called him a rising star.

Snapshot

⭐ **Name**: Shia Saide LaBeouf

⭐ **Birthday**: June 11, 1986

⭐ **Birthplace**: Los Angeles, California

⭐ **Home**: Burbank, California

⭐ **Appearances**: *Even Stevens, Holes, Charlie's Angels: Full Throttle, The Battle of Shaker Heights, I, Robot, The Greatest Game Ever Played, Disturbia, Surf's Up, Transformers, Indiana Jones and the Kingdom of the Crystal Skull, Eagle Eye, Transformers 2*

Important Words

comedian a person who uses funny talk and actions to make people laugh.

commercial (kuh-MUHR-shuhl) a short message on television or radio that helps sell a product.

debut (DAY-byoo) a first appearance.

future (FYOO-chuhr) a time that has not yet occurred.

international (ihn-tuhr-NASH-nuhl) of or relating to more than one nation.

professional (pruh-FEHSH-nuhl) working for money rather than for pleasure.

role a part an actor plays in a show.

stunt an action requiring great skill or daring.

Web Sites

To learn more about Shia LaBeouf, visit ABDO Publishing Company on the World Wide Web. Web sites about Shia LaBeouf are featured on our Book Links page. These links are routinely monitored and updated to provide the most current information available.

www.abdopublishing.com

Index